The
TECUMSEH
You Never Knew

BY JAMES LINCOLN COLLIER

Children's Press®
A Division of Scholastic Inc.
New York Toronto London Auckland Sydney
Mexico City New Delhi Hong Kong
Danbury, Connecticut

Library of Congress Cataloging-in-Publication Data

Collier, James Lincoln, 1928-
  The Tecumseh you never knew / James Lincoln Collier ; [illustrations by Greg Copeland].
    v. cm.
  Includes bibliographical references and index.
  Contents: An Indian boy grows up — The war heats up — Rebuilding the confederacy — Tippecanoe — Triumph and tragedy.
  ISBN 0-516-24426-4
  1. Tecumseh, Shawnee Chief, 1768-1813—Juvenile literature. 2. Shawnee Indians—Kings and rulers—Biography—Juvenile literature. [1. Tecumseh, Shawnee Chief, 1768-1813. 2. Shawnee Indians—Biography. 3. Indians of North America—East (U.S.)—Biography. 4. Kings, queens, rulers, etc.] I. Copeland, Greg, ill. II. Title.
  E99.S35T1153 2004
  974.004'97317'0092—dc22

2003028205

Illustrations by Greg Copeland
Book design by A. Natacha Pimentel C.

Photographs © 2004: Art Resource, NY: 9, 37, 47 (National Portrait Gallery, Smithsonian Institution, Washington, DC), 1, 34 (Delaware Art Museum, Wilmington, USA, Louisa DuPont Copeland Memorial Fund); Corbis Images/Bettmann: 26, 54, 55, 62, 74; National Archives of Canada: 19 (C-011014), 21 (C-040109); Collection of The New York Historical Society (41012): 7; North Wind Picture Archives: cover, 4, 12, 29, 30, 39, 45, 48, 52, 59, 65, 68, 69, 72; Ohio Historical Society: 32, 33 (SC404), 13; PictureHistory.com: 16.

CONTENTS

Chapter 1

AN INDIAN BOY GROWS UP

THERE HAVE BEEN MANY GREAT Native American heroes—Sitting Bull, Geronimo, Crazy Horse, Osceola, and Joseph Brant, to name a few. But almost everybody, both Indians and non-Indians, agrees that the greatest of them all—that we know of—is Tecumseh. Like many Indian leaders, he was fearless in battle. And like many, he was determined to save his land and his people from the American settlers. But Tecumseh, more than any of the others, worked out a realistic plan for keeping the settlers out of Indian lands, and he came closer to doing it than any other.

Tecumseh, perhaps the greatest of Native American heroes

There was something about Tecumseh that made people admire him. Shining out of him were personal qualities of honor, decency, bravery, fortitude, and intelligence. Sitting Bull, perhaps the next most important Indian leader, was admired by many and hated by many, but even Tecumseh's white enemies praised him in the highest terms. One man who fought him, William Henry Harrison, who later became president of the United States, called him an uncommon genius. Harrison said that in other circumstances Tecumseh would have been "the founder of an empire."

Tecumseh was born in 1768 or thereabouts. It is important for us to remember that what would soon become the United States of America was still a collection of colonies controlled by the British. The British also controlled Canada. By 1768 Americans were discontent under British rule. Many were beginning to talk about breaking free from the British empire. As early as 1765 Americans rioted against the notorious British stamp tax.

This conflict between the Americans and the British would play a major role in Tecumseh's life. The Indians did not really care very much who ruled North America. But some saw how tension between the European nations could be used to the Indians' advantage. In truth, as Tecumseh would discover while growing up, there was no way for the Indians to avoid being drawn into the struggle. It would become a key element in Tecumseh's life.

Tecumseh's parents were members of the Shawnee tribe. They had lived in the South, but by the time Tecumseh was born they were living near what is now Chillicothe, Ohio. His name meant "comet," or "shooting star," although some believe that it also meant "panther crouching for its prey."

A typical Shawnee dwelling. Made of mats laid over a wooden frame, it was easy to take down and move. Women usually did the gardening and prepared the food. Here they are boiling down maple sap to make sugar.

Tecumseh had several brothers and sisters. Like most Indian children of his time, he began life strapped to a cradleboard, which could be easily carried around by his mother or hung from the branch of a tree when she was busy with her chores. The Shawnee villages he lived in usually had anywhere from a hundred to several hundred people. The women did much of the routine work. They raised corn, beans, squash, and pumpkins in their gardens, picked wild berries in season, and made maple sugar from maple tree sap in the spring. They also built the shelters for their families. These were made by digging posts in the ground and then covering them with bark or skins. There was little furniture in such houses, mainly platforms that served as beds, tables, and chairs.

In winter, life was more difficult. When the cold weather and snow came, each family went off into the woods to live in temporary homes of skins thrown over poles. The men hunted. If hunting was good, the family ate well. If it was not, they sometimes went hungry. In spring the Shawnees were often thin and eager for the coming of warm weather.

Like all Indian boys, Tecumseh was trained to hunt from childhood. By the time he was born, Indians had gotten guns from whites, along with steel tools and

This imaginative portrait of Tecumseh was published in Germany after his death. His fame had spread around Europe as well as America.

weapons. Nonetheless, they still used traditional weapons like bows and arrows, tomahawks, spears, and clubs. Indian boys were expected to become expert with these, too.

Even as a boy, Tecumseh showed a special gift for hunting. Once, when he was around twelve, he and another boy saw two or three buffaloes by a stream. (There were still buffaloes in the East at the time.) They killed them and cut them up. When their chief saw what they had done, he was angry, for he had told them not to hunt by the stream. He struck Tecumseh and the other boy across the back with a rod.

Tecumseh was embarrassed, but he was determined to show the chief that he was a good hunter. The next day he and the other boy went out hunting again. Soon they heard other hunters chasing buffaloes toward them.

They climbed into a tree and waited for the buffaloes to come along. The other boy had a gun that could fire only one shot before being reloaded. Tecumseh had a bow. He shot his arrows rapidly into the buffalo herd as it passed under him and killed sixteen of them. This time the chief praised him for his good work.

This story illustrates an important point about the Indians of Tecumseh's time. Before the coming of the Europeans, the Native Americans had been self-sufficient: anything they needed they made, grew, or caught for themselves. But the Europeans brought with them a lot of things that the Indians did not know how to make, like woven cloth, metal tools and weapons, guns, metal needles, thread, and iron cooking pots. The Indians soon discovered that they could trade animal furs and skins for these things. A big trade built up between the Indians and the Europeans. Trading was particularly brisk with the British in Canada, but it went on with the American settlers, too. This trade pulled the Indians into friendly relations with many whites. Obviously, the Indians could not be fighting with them all the time if they wished to go on trading for guns, ammunition, and other goods.

And yet the Indians were faced with the fact that the settlers were constantly pushing into Indian territory. Europeans had been doing this since they first came to North America. Back in Europe, and especially in England, the population was growing. Many British people were finding it hard to get jobs or land to farm. The solution for them was to come to America.

As the American population grew, new settlers pushed farther and farther west in search of fertile land, frequently ignoring Indian claims to it. Here a wagon train moves through Indian hunting grounds.

By Tecumseh's time, Europeans had been farming the land along the east coast for 150 years. The soil was growing thin. The land was overpopulated. The forests needed for lumber and firewood were being cut down.

But over the Allegheny Mountains there were endless miles of forests and millions of acres of fertile land, all washed by clear rivers and streams. This area, roughly what is now Ohio, Indiana, and portions of the nearby states, was at the time called the Northwest Territory. As Tecumseh was growing up, the English settlers were rolling into the land claimed by his

Shawnee people and other tribes. The settlers did not really intend to harm the Native Americans, but they cut down the forests to grow their crops. Inevitably the deer, buffalo, and other game the Indians depended upon for food moved away. For the Indians, the inrush of settlers was a disaster.

But there wasn't much they could do about it. There were several problems, but among the worst

A typical frontier farm. Trees were cut, leaving the stumps in the field. The house was built of the logs, and the fences were made of split logs. Settlers rapidly cut down the forest, which supported the deer, bear, and other animals the Indians used for food.

were the fierce rivalries that existed among many Native American tribes. Some of these rivalries had existed for a century or more. The result was that often it was more important for an Indian tribe to battle its Indian rival than to fight off the land-hungry settlers.

For example, in the year Tecumseh was born, the Iroquois of New York claimed they owned a lot of the Northwest even though they did not live there. They had won it, the Iroquois said, in a fight a hundred years earlier. They decided they would sell some of it to the British. So a deal was made, and the British got Kentucky, much of western Pennsylvania, and more. The Iroquois did not even give any of the money from the sale to the Shawnees and other Native Americans living there.

This land held important hunting grounds for the Shawnees and other tribes. Of course they refused to accept the deal, but the Shawnees had only about a thousand people in the area, including only three hundred or so warriors, and were not strong enough to fight for it.

They saw clearly that if the settlers were to be kept out of the Northwest Territory, the Indian tribes would have to join together. If they pooled their warriors, they might have an army large enough to defeat the settlers. The Shawnees sent out messengers, urging the tribes to put aside their quarrels and fight together. The Indians should be "all of one mind and one color."

But they couldn't do it. The old hatreds between tribes were too strong. Friction between the settlers and the Indians grew. Some Native Americans were killed and so were some settlers. In the end the governor of Virginia put together a small army to drive the Indians out. He burned some Shawnee villages. The Shawnees decided to fight back, even though the governor's army was really too large for them to take on. The Shawnees pulled all their people together, and in October 1774 they attacked. Two of the people in the Shawnee war party were Tecumseh's father and his older brother, Cheeseekau.

One settler who was at the battle said, "I cannot describe the bravery of the [Indians] in the battle. It exceeded every man's expectations." Again and again, the Indians charged the settlers' lines, only to be driven back. Finally the Indian chiefs saw that they could not win and pulled back. But on the battlefield, Tecumseh's father lay dying. With his last breaths he told Tecumseh's brother Cheeseekau that he must preserve the honor of the family and lead his younger brother into battle against the whites.

Chapter 2

THE WAR HEATS UP

MEANWHILE, SOMETHING OF GREAT consequence not only to Tecumseh and the Native Americans, but for America, was taking place. As students of history know, in 1775 American minutemen and British soldiers fought the famous Battle of Concord and Lexington, which started the American Revolution. All the years when Tecumseh was a teenager the Americans and British fought from Massachusetts down to South Carolina without either side being able to win.

This picture of Tecumseh, from 1800, is somewhat fanciful, but suggests how well known this Indian hero was among whites.

Most of the fighting in the American Revolution was in the East near the Atlantic Coast, where most settlers lived. The British still held Canada, which did not rebel, and the Northwest Territory was being disputed by Americans, British, and Indians.

Both sides in the Revolution wanted to bring the Indians in on their side, or at least keep them neutral. There were conferences and peace talks. Some Indians tended to side with the American settlers. But most did not—particularly the Indians in the Northwest Territory, such as the Shawnees, who had long been trading with the British around the Great Lakes. The British had been the Shawnees' main source for guns, gunpowder, and shot (as bullets were called). Whatever the Indians thought about Europeans, they could not afford to break off their trade with them. Therefore through the years of the Revolution there continued to be a lot of fighting—Indians against Indians, Indians against Americans or British.

In 1781 the Americans won a great victory at Yorktown, and the war was mainly over. However, the peace treaty was not signed until 1783. It is important to understand that the treaty required the British to leave their forts around the Great Lakes. It also required the Americans to pay certain debts to the British.

The British, however, did not want to give up their Great Lakes forts. They believed that the American government was weak and that the new United States of America would soon fall apart. When that happened they would swoop down from their Great Lakes forts and retake the Northwest Territory with its rich lands and abundant furs. As it happened, the Americans were slow to pay the debts ordered by the treaty. The British used that as an excuse to linger in their forts.

Furs were one of the major exports from North America to Europe. Beaver was particularly important, for its fur was used to make the hats many American and European men wore. This picture shows Indians exchanging furs for money and goods with British traders.

But the British had a complicated political problem. They wanted to stay on friendly terms with the Indians, partly for trade, and partly to keep them as allies, if needed. On the other hand, they did not yet want to get into another war with the Americans. They had problems elsewhere in the world they had to deal with. They could not really encourage the Indians to go to war against the Americans, for fear of getting drawn in themselves. For the British, it was going to be a tricky balancing act.

The Americans had no such problems. Full of confidence after their victory in the Revolution, they insisted that they had won the Northwest Territory in the war from both the British *and* the Indians. It was theirs to do what they wanted with, and what they wanted was to fill it with settlers.

The Indians saw this. More and more they began to see that they must pull together if they were to have any chance of stopping the flood of settlers.

In 1783 the leaders of many tribes met at a village on the Lower Sandusky River south of Lake Erie to organize their defense. They made an important decision that no tribe could sell any land to the settlers unless the whole Indian confederacy agreed to it. The land belonged to them all. It was "a dish with one spoon."

The most important Indian leader in this movement was the Mohawk chief Joseph Brant. He understood that the settlers would try to pin the tribes against one another, and he saw that the Indians must not let them do this.

By this time Tecumseh, still a teenager, was becoming a warrior. His start was not very glorious. At fourteen, his much-admired older brother, Cheeseekau, allowed him to join a battle party. There was a skirmish in the woods. Cheeseekau was hit, although not seriously wounded. "Momentarily confused and shocked by the bloodshed, Tecumseh abandoned his position and fled panic-stricken through the forest," says one historian. Humiliated, he vowed that such a thing would never happen again. It never did.

Before Tecumseh, Joseph Brant (pictured here) was the most important Indian leader. Like Tecumseh, Brant knew that the Indians had to stick together if they were to have a chance against the white settlers.

As great a warrior as Tecumseh would become, there was another side to his personality. One man who knew him said that he was "free-hearted and generous to excess, always ready to relieve the wants of others. When he returned from a hunting expedition he would harangue his companions . . . to instill into their minds honorable and humane sentiments." If somebody admired one of Tecumseh's tomahawks, he would instantly give it to him.

He showed this compassion toward his enemies, too. Among the Indians the rule was that a prisoner belonged to the person who captured him. Sometimes prisoners, especially if they were young, were adopted into the tribe. Sometimes they were let go. But in many cases they were executed or even tortured to death. The tortures could be fearsome. The prisoner's tongue might be cut out. His bones might be broken slowly, one at a time. Finally he would be burned alive or, if he was lucky, his skull split with a tomahawk.

To the Indians these practices were normal. Warriors captured in battle expected to be tortured. They were supposed to show bravery during the torture and not flinch or cry out. In many tribes young boys would learn brave songs to sing while they were being burned to death. The settlers, however, thought the torturing of prisoners was barbarous, and came to believe that the Indians were brutal savages who deserved no mercy. Often they did not spare women and children in the fighting—nor did the Indians. This frontier warfare was very cruel to everybody.

Tecumseh came to believe that the torture of prisoners was unnecessary. In one battle some prisoners were taken. Some were ransomed. Others, however, were beaten to death or burned alive. Watching one victim dying in agony, Tecumseh was touched and saddened. After the dreadful sight was finished, he exhorted his followers not to slaughter any more prisoners. So convincing was he that the warriors agreed to it. In battle Tecumseh could be fierce and do his enemies no kindness. But killing helpless prisoners was another matter. Again and again through his life he tried to save them, and often he did.

Between his skill and daring as a fighter, his frankness and honesty, his intelligence, and his compassion and generosity, Tecumseh's reputation grew. More and more Indians began to hear of him, and in time he gathered a following of about ten warriors, making him a minor chief. He was not as important as his older brother, Cheeseekau, who commanded thirty warriors, but his fame was increasing.

During the years after the British-American peace treaty of 1783, the Indians struggled to work together. Sometimes they succeeded, sometimes not. But year after year they battled the settlers.

Tecumseh was always in the thick of the fighting. Once, some Kentuckians attacked the camp where he and some warriors were sleeping. Tecumseh snatched up his war club even as he was waking up and charged a group of Kentuckians equipped with guns. He killed one of them, and the Kentuckians, convinced that they were fighting a much larger party, fled. One who knew Tecumseh said that he was "proud, courageous, and high-spirited, would never yield, but would any time fight double his numbers. . . . He always inspired his companions with confidence and valor."

Ironically, Tecumseh missed one of the most important battles of the time. In 1791 the American Congress, determined to stop the Indians from threatening the settlers, voted to spend the money to create a large attack force. The force would be led by Arthur St. Clair, governor of the Northwest Territory. By October St. Clair had his army on the march and was moving into western Ohio.

But the Indians, too, had assembled an army, drawing on warriors from many tribes. They were now well supplied with arms by the British. According to one report, Tecumseh was out with a small party of scouts to watch St. Clair's army as it moved through the woods. The Indians closed in and waited. At dawn of November 4, 1791, they encircled St. Clair's camp and suddenly struck. A hail of gunfire fell upon the American soldiers as they were cooking breakfast. Some panicked and fell back on the rest. Other soldiers held their ground and fired back at the Indians, but they were shooting at an enemy well hidden in the woods. One after another the Indians picked the whites off.

Finally St. Clair had had enough. He pulled his forces together, and they broke through the Indian lines and fled in disorder through the woods. The Indians suffered about 150 casualties in the fight, but 647 white soldiers lay dead on the battlefield, and hundreds more were wounded.

This great victory over a strong white army vastly encouraged the Indians. They came to think that if they held the confederacy together, they could drive the whites out of the Northwest Territory. They geared up to fight.

Arthur St. Clair was important in the fight against the British during the Revolution and went on to become governor of the Northwest Territory. It was his job to pacify the Indians and to keep them from harming the settlers.

At one meeting, when there was an argument over making a certain attack, Cheeseekau arose, stretched out his hands, and according to one report said, "With these hands I have taken the lives of three hundred men, and now the time is come when they shall take the lives of three hundred more. Then I will be satisfied and sit down in peace. I will now drink my fill of blood."

Tecumseh went with his brother into this battle, bringing his warriors. A few days before the fight Cheeseekau told the others that he had dreamed of the battle. In his dream he was shot in the head. The Indians strongly believed in the power of dreams to foretell the future. Many of them urged Cheeseekau to stay out of the fight, but he would not. It was an "honor to die in battle," he said.

A few days later they came to a small fort. It was night, but a bright moon lit up the area. The Indians creeped toward the fort. Then some cattle grazing outside the walls saw the silent figures slipping through the trees. They broke and ran, bellowing. A man inside the fort heard the noise and peered out through a loophole. He saw the Indians in the shadowy moonlight. The man fired. The bullet caught Cheeseekau in the forehead, and he dropped dead.

For Tecumseh the death of his brother was a tragedy. Cheeseekau had been father and older brother combined, the man who had taught him how to hunt, who had infused him with the spirit of bravery and honor. Tecumseh was now more than ever determined to drive the white settlers out of the Indians' lands.

The United States government, however, was equally determined to finish off the Indian threat. The War Department sent out another army, this one commanded by one of the best generals it had, Anthony Wayne. He had fought resourcefully against the British in the Revolution, and had become known as "Mad" Anthony Wayne, for his daring.

Wayne brought his army into the Northwest Territory and built a series of forts through the area to give him a string of bases to operate from. The Indians decided to attack one of these forts when Wayne was away with the main army. At dawn on June 30, 1794, they attacked. At first they beat the Americans back, but they could not break into the fort.

Then General Wayne came up with his main army. The Indians formed a defensive line in an area of the woods where a lot of trees had been blown down by a tornado. The spot was known as Fallen Timbers. Tecumseh's warriors were on the left of the Indian defensive line.

"Mad" Anthony Wayne was one of the best generals George Washington had during the Revolution. Wayne's victory over the Indians in the Battle of Fallen Timbers discouraged them in their fight to keep the settlers out.

At first the Indians pushed the attackers back. But then a contingent of mounted troops charged, flashing their swords. Behind them came the infantry. The Indians were vastly outnumbered. Tecumseh fought courageously. For awhile he was able to hold his position, his warriors picking off Wayne's men as they pushed forward. But then Wayne ordered a flanking movement to get around the side of the Indian line.

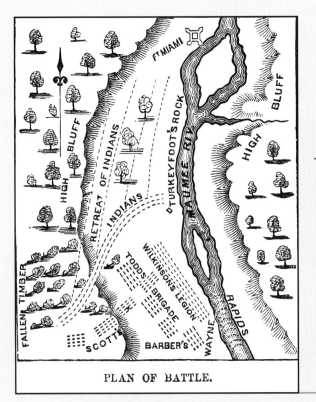

PLAN OF BATTLE.

Tecumseh and his Indian followers fought with great bravery at Fallen Timbers, but they were outnumbered and had to fall back. The Indians tended to fight in a helter-skelter way, which hurt them against the disciplined troops, who used careful tactics.

The Indians were now forced to fall back in order to avoid being encircled. Soon they were retreating through the forest.

The Battle of Fallen Timbers was lost. The Indians retreated until they reached one of the forts of the British, who had been supplying them with arms. They asked the commander of the fort to open the gates for them.

The British commander did not know what to do. The Indians were friends of the British. However, if he let them into the fort, the Americans might attack it and start a war between America and Great Britain. The commander knew that the British government did not want this. So he kept the doors closed. According to one report he shouted down, "I cannot let you in. You are painted too much, my children," meaning that they had on war paint. The Indians turned away and established a new base. But Tecumseh now knew that he could not entirely trust the English.

The Battle of Fallen Timbers was important, for it led many Indians to believe that they could never beat the whites. Some of them decided that they had better try to make peace. Indeed, some believed that they had better side with the Americans against the British if it came to a war.

After Fallen Timbers, many Indians felt that the Americans could not be beaten. They were willing to negotiate with Wayne for the best deal they could get. At a meeting at Fort Greenville, they gave away about two-thirds of Ohio for goods worth a fraction of the value of the land. This picture shows Wayne in front of the fort as the treaty is being signed.

So in the summer of 1795, a group of dispirited Indian chiefs met with General Wayne in Fort Greenville. They agreed to give about two-thirds of what is now Ohio, as well as part of Indiana, to the Americans. They were given $20,000 worth of goods and would be allowed to hunt on the land they had given away. But these hunting rights would not matter, for over time white settlers would cut down the forest and drive away the game.

The great confederacy that had beaten St. Clair had fallen apart. But Tecumseh remembered it, and he remembered the deaths of his father and his brother at the hands of the settlers. Other chiefs might surrender, Tecumseh would not.

Chapter 3

REBUILDING THE CONFEDERACY

WE SHOULDN'T THINK THAT THE Indians were the only people who fought so much among themselves. In Europe, nations small and large had been fighting among themselves for several thousand years. The same was true of African tribes and of many people elsewhere. But for the Indians, the inability to pull together was crucial, for they were faced by a larger and better-armed challenger.

An artist's idea of Tecumseh speaking to American settlers in the endless conflict over Indian lands

Tecumseh recognized this. He was well aware that unless the Indians could form another confederacy they had no hope against the settlers. But he also knew that the Indians were not yet ready to fight. Too many Indians had decided to "walk the white man's road," take up farming, and try to get along with the settlers.

The Indians had now come to respect him greatly. He established himself as the chief of his own village and bided his time. Despite the new boundaries drawn at the Greenville Treaty, whites continued to cross the line into Indian territory to carve out farms. In response, Tecumseh moved his village farther west, and farther west again, finally landing in what is now central Indiana. There seemed to be nothing else he could do without the cooperation of other tribes.

Curiously, the seed for a new confederacy was planted, not by Tecumseh, but by his younger brother, Lalawethika. This brother certainly did not look like a leader, nor act like one, either. According to one historian, he had a "hangdog look, reduced frame, and disfigured right eye," due to an accident. Nor was he popular with the other Indians—"a talkative, blustering, noisy fellow, full of deceit." He had never shown much bravery in battle, and had at least once fled during a fight. He was not a very good hunter, either.

And yet he would become one of the most famous Indians of his day, although hardly the most respected.

Despite all this, Lalawethika was smart and very clever with words. He took up the profession of "healer"—a person who knew the kinds of roots and herbs that cured certain illnesses. (Not all of these Indian folk medicines worked, but many of them did, as modern scientists have discovered.)

The Indians also believed—as did people in many cultures—that evil spirits were responsible for many illnesses. Lalawethika knew prayers and rituals that were believed to drive away evil spirits.

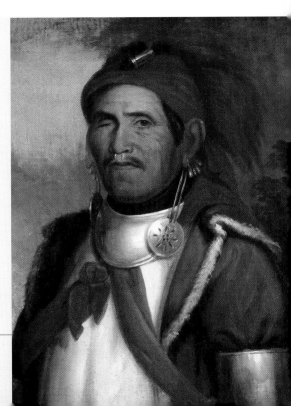

The Prophet, also called Lalawethika and Tenskwatawa. He lacked physical courage but was smart. As this picture shows, one of his eyes had been damaged when he was young. He preached keeping Indian ways, but sometimes himself wore white man's clothing.

As a healer, Lalawethika gained a certain respect from other Shawnees. Nonetheless, he remained a lazy man, one who was not eager to go into battle. He also had a fondness for whiskey.

Indians sometimes traded furs and skins for whiskey. Whiskey was cheap, and white traders were glad to swap it for furs rather than giving the Indians guns, which they might use against settlers. Unfortunately, many Indians proved to have little tolerance for alcohol, and very soon alcoholism came to be a major problem in many Indian villages. It became a problem for Lalawethika, too.

In April 1805 he had a frightening dream that showed him the fate of Indians who lived bad lives. In his dream he heard the souls of such people "roaring like the falls of a river" as they suffered agonizing punishment after death. Lalawethika awoke from the dream a different person. Like the people in his dream, he had been living a bad life. He knew he must reform. Not only did he reform himself, but he began urging other Indians to reform as well. He began to preach to them, "his body trembling with emotion and his eyes wet with tears," according to one historian. The Indians, he said, must give up white man's whiskey. They must learn to be kind to their wives and children. They must be honest and fair to one another.

Most important for our story, Lalawethika said that the Great Spirit had always meant for the Indians and whites to remain separate. Indians should use bows and arrows instead of guns, should dress in skins instead of cloth, should not keep animals—like cats and cows—brought to them by whites. They should go back to their old ways and live by hunting, and growing corn, beans, and melons.

This early woodcut shows an artist's idea of the Prophet in a mystic ceremony. Whites were very interested in Indian practices. Some supported the Indians' rights to their land, but most Americans saw the Indians as a dangerous threat.

As Lalawethika preached to more people, his fame spread. He took a new name, Tenskwatawa, meaning "the Open Door." Soon he was also being called the Prophet. Naturally, one of the Indians who was interested was his older brother, Tecumseh. The Prophet's teaching fit much of what Tecumseh already believed—that the less the Indians had to do with whites, the better. He began wearing ceremonial Indian clothes made of deerskin instead of shirts and trousers made of the white people's cloth.

But Tecumseh was a realistic man with a far-reaching vision. He realized that if the Indians gave up guns and steel knives they would be at a terrible disadvantage in battles against whites. He kept his weapons.

How much Tecumseh really believed that his younger brother was truly a prophet with a message from the Great Spirit is hard to say. He probably took the story with a grain of salt. But he saw very clearly that the Prophet could be very useful in bringing Indians together. The Prophet's message was meant not for the Shawnees alone, but for all Indians. Here was an opportunity to rebuild the confederacy.

So together the two brothers went from village to village, arguing their case for unity. Many village chiefs, jealous of their power, refused to bring their people in under Tecumseh and the Prophet, but many others did. And in 1806 the two brothers began building a village where Indians of all tribes could come together and live according to the teachings of the Prophet.

Tecumseh, however, was not aiming for war with the whites. One of the keys to intelligence is the ability to look beyond your own feelings. While he might like to

take revenge on the whites for taking away the Indians' land, Tecumseh saw that the most important thing was for the Indians to be separate from whites so they could live in their own ways. Besides, the Indians were not yet ready for a fight. He would be content to live in peace if the settlers would let them.

However, it did not seem that the settlers would let them. Land hunger was strong among them. Tens of thousands of immigrants were pouring into the United States, mainly from the British Isles, and many of them were coming into the Northwest. Some Indians ignored the beliefs of Joseph Brant and others that the land should belong to all Indians—"a dish with one spoon," as Brant put it. They sold land to settlers. Tecumseh of course hated these land sales, but often there was little he could do about them. Such sales left many young Indians embittered, though, and they were ready to join Tecumseh to defend Indian land. But Tecumseh saw that the time was still not right. He had to rebuild the confederacy first. As the number of settlers grew, Tecumseh was forced to move again. In 1808 he and the Prophet moved to the junction of the Tippecanoe and Wabash rivers in what is now Indiana. Here they built a village called Prophetstown. Supporters of their cause began to flood in.

Then, once again, bad feelings between the British and Americans erupted, and the Indians were drawn in. When two gangs get into a fight, people around them are likely to be hurt—this was what happened to the Indians.

The issues upsetting the British and Americans were complicated. For one, the British navy was short of men, and often stopped American merchant ships and took away their sailors, claiming that they were British deserters. For another, the British still refused to get out of the forts on the Great Lakes. Finally, many Americans believed that the British were giving the Indians guns and gunpowder and urging them to slaughter American settlers in the Northwest. It was probably not true that the British were urging the Indians to kill American settlers, but it is certainly true that they were supplying them with weapons.

For their part, the British were worried that the Americans might try to conquer Canada. The British Empire remained mighty, but Canada had a long border that was poorly defended. Inevitably, both sides realized that the Indians could be important allies.

But Tecumseh wanted to stay out of it. All he wanted was peace. He went to several conferences with both British and American officials. At these conferences he insisted that he had no wish to fight anybody. He simply wanted the whites to stay out of Indian lands. In 1808 a British report said:

> *The Prophet's brother, who is stated to me to be his principle support and who appears to be a very shrewd intelligent man . . . was endeavoring to collect the different nations to form one settlement on the Wabash [Prophetstown] . . . in order to preserve their country from all encroachments. Their intention is not to take part in the quarrels: that if the Americans encroach on them they are resolved to strike—but he added that if their father the King [of England] should be in earnest and appear in sufficient force they would hold fast to him.*

Tecumseh was saying that if everybody left him and his people alone there would be no trouble. However if the Americans tried to drive them out he would join with the British, provided the British would back up the Indians with ammunition and troops.

The British in turn said that they did not wish a war with the United States. They had enough problems in other parts of the world. They would not encourage the Indians to start trouble with the Americans.

However, if war did come, they would welcome Tecumseh's help. Meanwhile, they would continue to supply the Indians with guns, powder, and, when necessary, food.

By this time Tecumseh was taking charge of the Indian cause. The Prophet was still more famous, but Tecumseh knew that his brother was too weak a person to lead his people. Tecumseh now began telling the Prophet what he wanted him to do. At one point Tecumseh even threatened to kill him for going against his wishes. The Prophet was aware that his brother was the far wiser person and accepted Tecumseh's rule.

At first the Prophet was the head of the Indian movement, but soon Tecumseh became the main leader. At times he became very angry with the Prophet for disobeying his orders, as shown in this picture.

Tecumseh was now traveling far and wide trying to convince the Indians that they must stand together in order to hold off the land-hungry Americans. He went deep into the South to talk to the Creeks and Cherokees, up into Michigan to meet with the Potawatomis and Ottawas, into Ohio to see the Wyandots. He did not always persuade other Indians to join his confederacy, but often he did. Many of them moved to Prophetstown, especially young warriors eager for glory. A few years before, nobody but his own Shawnees had heard of Tecumseh. Now he was talked about by everyone— Indian, American, and British.

Then, in 1809, the governor of the Indiana Territory, where Prophetstown was, made a decision that would have serious effects on everyone. The governor was William Henry Harrison, a young general who would later become president of the United States partly because of what was about to happen. Harrison was an ambitious man who had little use for the Indians. He wanted to build up the population of Indiana, and that meant taking over more Indian land. He called a conference of Indians at Fort Wayne, to which more than a thousand came. Tecumseh was away trying to bring people into his confederacy and did not attend. At the conference Harrison offered to buy from the

Indians three million acres of land, an area larger than the present state of Connecticut. For this he offered the Indians less than two cents an acre.

The largest group of Indians there were the Potawatomis. The game in their area had been nearly exhausted, and they were living in poverty. Unfortunately, the Potawatomis had no claim to the land Harrison wanted to buy, as Harrison well knew. Nonetheless, the Potawatomis, eager for money and trade goods, urged the other Indians at the meeting to go along. Harrison cajoled, badgered, threatened, and argued. In the end the Indians gave in. Harrison bought most of the southern part of Indiana for what the Americans considered a laughable amount of money. Yet again, the Indians' failure to pull together had cost them dearly.

William Henry Harrison believed in taking a tough position against the Indians. His victory at the Battle of Tippecanoe made him a hero to many Americans, and in time he was elected president.

Chapter 4

TIPPECANOE

W HEN TECUMSEH RETURNED FROM
his trip and found out about the treaty of Fort
Wayne, he was furious. Tecumseh was angry at
both Harrison for taking advantage of the starving
Potawatomis, and with the Indians who had
signed the treaty. He said flatly that he was prepared to kill white settlers coming into the area
granted by the Fort Wayne Treaty. It was now
clear in his mind that the Americans could not
be trusted. The Indians would have to fight.

This is an artist's idea of the Battle of Tippecanoe.

Tecumseh redoubled his efforts to pull as many Indians as he could into the confederacy. In many cases, he believed, weak or treacherous chiefs were the problem. He went around to their villages with his warriors and asked such chiefs to resign. If they did not, he ruthlessly removed them from power. Again and again Tecumseh argued his case for an alliance. If the Indians stuck together they could hold off the American settlers.

In his heart he knew it would come to war. He visited the British in their Great Lakes forts, telling them this. The British, as usual, played their balancing act. Yes, they would fight with the Indians if it came to war; but no, they would do nothing to trigger a war which might cost them Canada, as it nearly did. But nothing would stop Tecumseh. He had set his life on preserving Indian lands and their way of life.

Governor Harrison knew what Tecumseh was doing. Many Indians remained friendly to the Americans and would tell them things. American traders, too, went into Indian villages, and they heard gossip about Tecumseh's plans.

Harrison also knew how important Tecumseh was to the Indians. He wrote:

The implicit obedience and respect which the followers of Tecumseh pay to him is really astonishing and more than any other circumstance bespeaks him one of those uncommon geniuses, which spring up occasionally to produce revolutions and overturn the established order of things. . . . No difficulties deter him. . . . For four years he has been in constant motion. You see him today on the Wabash and in a short time you hear of him on the shores of Lake Erie or Michigan, or on the banks of the Mississippi and wherever he goes he makes an impression favorable to his purpose.

Harrison now asked Tecumseh to meet with him. Tecumseh agreed to come. The meeting was tense. Both Harrison and Tecumseh were surrounded by armed warriors. Tecumseh insisted that he wanted peace, but that he also wanted Indian lands left alone. Harrison insisted that the Indiana land had been legally sold according to the Fort Wayne Treaty.

Then Tecumseh made a mistake. He asked Governor Harrison to keep the settlers out of the treaty land for the moment. He himself was going south to bring back many warriors, and they would need the land to hunt on for food. He added that once he had returned he would visit the president of the United States and settle matters. For the moment, he wished things to stay as they were.

The meeting ended with nothing settled, but Harrison now saw his chance. While Tecumseh was away he would attack Prophetstown and destroy it, thus eliminating Tecumseh's main base of operations.

With Tecumseh traveling, the Prophet was in charge. It is possible that Tecumseh could have figured out a way to head off Harrison, but the Prophet could not.

Tecumseh and Harrison met at least twice to work out their difficulties. At one of these meetings tempers grew hot. Harrison drew his sword, and the soldiers with him raised their weapons. Fortunately, Harrison was able to cool things down before there was bloodshed.

In September 1811 Harrison marched off with more than a thousand men, headed for Prophetstown. He stopped to build a fort and then set off again. By early November he was closing in on his goal. During this long march, the Indians might have attacked the American troops from ambush. They did not. Had Tecumseh been there things might have been done differently.

When the Americans came close to Prophetstown, they stopped to camp, and Harrison sent out men with a white flag to arrange a conference. There was still some hope that matters could be settled peacefully. That night, however, the Indians got word that Harrison was going to attack the next day. They weren't sure the information was right, but the Indians decided not to take a chance. They would attack that night.

They were outnumbered—perhaps five hundred warriors against a thousand American troops. However, the Prophet told the warriors that the spirits would aid them. He said the Americans' gunpowder would turn to sand, and the Indians would become bulletproof. How many Indians believed this we do not know. In any case, they were dauntless and determined to make a fight of it. Very late at night they slipped out of Prophetstown. Dividing into two groups, they took up positions on opposite sides of the American camp.

Sometime before dawn an American sentry spotted an Indian and fired. The Battle of Tippecanoe was on. Giving a ferocious yell, the Indians charged through the darkness. The sentries turned and fled back into their lines. Soldiers began pouring out of their tents. Some were cut down by bullets before they could bring their guns into action. The Americans fell back.

Then Harrison and his aide leaped on their horses and rode into the battle. The aide was shot from his horse almost immediately and soon died. Whatever else might be said about the future president, William H. Harrison was cool in battle. He ordered up reinforcements, and organized his troops. The American line held.

The Indians, unable to break through, now began a series of quick attacks against the American lines.

Another view of the Battle of Tippecanoe. The Indians, who were low on ammunition, fled before Harrison's men charged at daybreak.

They would drive forward, fire their weapons, and retreat quickly to reload. For a time the two sides exchanged a torrent of bullets. The Indians, however, had an advantage. They were firing from the darkness of the woods, lit only by the moon. The Americans were outlined by their own campfires. Horsemen, profiled above ground in the firelight, suffered especially. One by one they were shot down.

William Henry Harrison became president of the United States in 1841. This romanticized picture of him as a great general astride a horse was probably drawn at the time of his presidential campaign.

But still the American line held. The Indians were beginning to use up their ammunition. Dawn was breaking, making them more visible to American troops. Harrison reorganized his men, and as the sky grew bright, they charged the Indians. Outnumbered and low on ammunition, the Indians had no choice but to flee, racing for Prophetstown, carrying with them as many dead and wounded as they could.

The Battle of Tippecanoe had lasted two and a half hours. The Americans had sixty-two dead and 120 wounded. The Indians lost perhaps fifty men. They had behaved with great courage in the face of a much stronger enemy. They had wounded the Americans enough so that Harrison kept his troops in camp for two days, preparing for a counterattack. When it did not come he cautiously took his troops out to Prophetstown. They found it deserted. They took the Indians' corn for their own use and burned the town.

The Battle of Tippecanoe was widely celebrated by Americans. At last the Indians had been beaten and their base of operations destroyed. The victory made William Henry Harrison a hero to Americans. Many years later he ran for the presidency, under the nickname Tippecanoe, and won, mainly due to his fame as an Indian-fighter.

Harrison now boasted that the Battle of Tippecanoe had ended the Indian threat. There would be peace on the frontier. He was reckoning without Tecumseh. For one thing, the Indians had not been utterly defeated at Tippecanoe, but had pulled out in the face of heavy odds. For another, Tecumseh's recruiting tour, which had taken him through the South and up the Mississippi into Illinois Territory and even Minnesota, had been successful. He had not been able to draw every tribe and village into his confederacy, but he had brought in a good many. He was building a powerful force.

It was truly a remarkable feat. Always, since the arrival of the whites in North America, the Indians had defeated themselves through their own rivalries and quarreling. Now, for a change, it looked as if they might pull together. Tecumseh was the leader of what may have been the largest confederation of Indians ever in North America.

We must realize that to accomplish this he had ridden or even walked through thousands of miles of wilderness, often living off the land. He had dealt with tribes who spoke many different languages, usually led by chiefs jealous of his power. Tecumseh was not merely a brave warrior, but a highly skilled diplomat able to get people to see things his way. By January 1812, when he returned to the ruins of Prophetstown, he was known as a great leader by everybody, both Indians and whites.

The Shawnees began rebuilding Prophetstown. Unfortunately, some were also determined to get revenge for the defeat at Tippecanoe. They attacked small settlements and secluded farms, sometimes killing whole families, including women and children. Tecumseh was strongly opposed to these raids. He did not want the settlers roused up until the confederacy was complete and he was ready to fight from strength.

In fact, other events were playing a role. The bad blood between England and the United States had grown worse. Americans were angry with the British for "kidnapping" their sailors, as the Americans saw it. They were also convinced that the British were encouraging the Indians to slaughter American settlers. In June 1812 the United States declared war on England. What we now call the War of 1812 had begun.

With war declared, the British could openly ally themselves with the Indians. For Tecumseh it was a natural idea. The Indians had long been trading with the British in Canada. The British had supplied them with weapons, which they needed not only for war but for hunting. There had been a measure of friendliness between them.

More important, it seemed that with the help of British troops and especially British cannon, they might be able to drive the American settlers out of the Northwest.

Tecumseh had, historians have estimated, several thousand warriors available to him. He was now ready to go to war. Historians are not quite sure what he was planning—he kept his plans secret. But it appears that southern Indians were to strike at Louisiana, while the northern tribes would attack settlements in Indiana and Illinois Territories.

The plans of the Americans were clearer. They were going to invade Canada. For one, they wanted to destroy the British forts around the Great Lakes, which since the Revolution had remained a threatening dagger over the Northwest Territory. For another, many Americans hoped that they could take over Canada and bring it into the United States. So an American force began to march toward the settlement of Detroit, to reinforce an American fort there.

The British and the Indians decided to attack the American army south of Detroit, near an Indian village called Monguaga. On August 9, 1812, at about four in the afternoon, the Americans appeared. They had many more troops than the British and Indians combined. The Indians set an ambush. At a signal from Tecumseh, a shot was fired. The Indians gave a terrible cry and began to shoot into the American ranks.

After one battle, some Indians began to slaughter a group of unarmed American prisoners. Enraged, Tecumseh rode among the Indians, demanding a halt to the killing. At right, an Indian scalps a dying American soldier.

Taken by surprise, the Americans were driven back. Soon, however, they pulled themselves together and began firing back. The British soldiers, in their bright red uniforms, were easy targets. The Indians, lying in the forest, were harder to hit. Bit by bit they gained ground.

Tecumseh fought, as he always did, with great daring. He kept urging his men on. The American general later said, "The Indians on the left, under the command of Tecumseh, fought with great obstinacy." But in the end the outnumbered British were forced to retreat. Without their support, Tecumseh had no choice but to follow. But the ferocious defense by Tecumseh and his warriors had made the Americans cautious, and they did not push the fight any further.

The Indians and the British, however, had been driven off. The Americans now proceeded to the fort at Detroit. But the American commander had been unnerved by the fight. Tecumseh and the British commander did not realize this. They were full of fight, and soon they advanced toward the American fort at Detroit. They were massing outside, when suddenly they saw a white flag waving from the walls of the fort. Unbelieving, they waited as American officers came out to them. They were even more astonished when the officers offered to surrender the fort.

Historians today have trouble understanding why the American commander gave up without a fight. As it happened, several hundred local settlers had gathered, with their families, in the fort for protection. Apparently the commander thought that the forces against him were very great. Also, the Indians might massacre everybody, women and children included, as they sometimes did after a victory. So he probably surrendered to avoid a massacre. Whatever the case, the commander was thrown out of the army in disgrace.

The Indians, thus, were important in stopping the invasion of Canada. Today Tecumseh is considered a hero there. If not for him, perhaps Canada would today be part of the United States.

Chapter 5
TRIUMPH AND TRAGEDY

WITH THE SURRENDER OF DETROIT the Indians had gained one of their greatest triumphs over the settlers. Tecumseh's farsighted idea that the Indians could win if they worked together was proving correct. Indians' confidence in themselves rose to a peak. Perhaps they really could, with British help, drive the settlers off their land.

The British general Proctor thought he had no choice but to retreat after the Americans gained control of Lake Erie. Tecumseh scorned retreat. The British had promised they would hold. He gave one of his most passionate speeches, during which he compared Proctor to a frightened animal.

But the Americans were not finished. The surrender of Detroit had embarrassed and enraged them. The American people were demanding that Detroit be retaken and the Indian menace be ended once and for all. More soldiers were sent out, and there was more fighting.

For the next several months the fighting seesawed. The Indians had some victories, but they suffered some defeats, too. Attacks on American forts usually failed. To bring down a fort they needed cannon to blast holes in the stockade walls. The Indians had no cannon of their own. They depended on British cannoneers, who unfortunately they often did not have.

A second problem was the Indian way of war. Over hundreds of years of warfare the Europeans had developed a system of war that utilized carefully worked-out tactics employing highly disciplined troops. For the Indians, warfare was mainly one-on-one. They would charge in disorder at the foe, each Indian picking out a single enemy to fight hand-to-hand. Such tactics rarely worked against a disciplined army. The Indians showed great courage and skill in battle, but it was not enough. In truth, the Indians could win only when they had the help of the British redcoats and, for various reasons, they did not always have the redcoats with them.

Tecumseh himself had a better understanding of European methods, but he could not always control his warriors, who fought for scalps, prisoners, and individual glory. Particularly troubling to Tecumseh was the Indian belief that prisoners belonged to whoever caught them. Tecumseh did not like to see the slaughter of helpless people. He also knew that the killing of prisoners enraged whites—not just the American enemies, but their British allies, as well.

An Indian attack during the War of 1812. The Indians won some victories, but in the end their one-on-one way of fighting could not work against disciplined troops.

After one victory by the British and the Indians, American prisoners were herded into a sort of pen. A few British soldiers were ordered to guard the prisoners, but some Indians, determined to take scalps, pushed the guards aside. They began shooting the prisoners or splitting their heads open with their tomahawks and scalping them. When one British guard protested, an Indian shot him dead. One of the prisoners later wrote, "A description is impossible. Without any means of defense or possibility of escape, death in all the horror of savage cruelty seemed to stare us in the face."

Suddenly Tecumseh and a British officer appeared. Tecumseh jumped onto the wall of the pen and angrily demanded that the Indians stop the massacre. His anger and authoritative manner was enough to halt the bloodletting. Later somebody who knew him wrote, "Never did Tecumseh shine more truly than on this occasion."

Nonetheless, Tecumseh was never able to control his Indian warriors as the whites could their own soldiers. For example, he had worked out a campaign for an Indian conquest of the South. He asked warriors there to hold off until he had things ready. But some hotheaded Indians would not wait, and attacked settlers, sometimes massacring women and children.

Inevitably, the Americans put together large forces and beat the Indians down village by village, where a common stand might have saved them. The southern part of the war soon ended.

Matters in the North seemed more hopeful. Control of the Great Lakes, especially Lake Erie, was a key to the defense of Canada. The Americans had ships in the lakes under the famous Commander Oliver Perry. The British had some ships of their own. On September 10, 1813, the two fleets met. Unfortunately for the British, their fleet was undermanned. The Americans won easily, and Perry sent a message to his chiefs that became famous: *We have met the enemy and they are ours.*

The Americans now had control of Lake Erie. They could prevent the British from moving troops and supplies around much of Canada by water, at a

The Battle of Lake Erie ended British control of the lake. At the center of this picture, the British ship Detroit is attacked by the American ship Caledonia. The Americans sank or captured all the British ships.

time when there were few roads through the forests. It also allowed the Americans to bombard British forts along the lake shores from their ships. The British commander felt that he had to pull his forces further inland to be out of reach of the American fleet.

Tecumseh was stunned and angry. His Indians had given much blood to help the British defend the area, and now the redcoats were walking away. On September 18 the British general finally faced the Indians at their council house. Tecumseh made a speech that is considered his greatest—perhaps the greatest speech ever made by an Indian that we know of.

You always told us you would never draw your foot off British ground. But now, father, we see you are drawing back, and we are sorry to see our father doing so without seeing the enemy. We must compare our father's conduct to a fat animal that carries its tail upon its back, but when affrighted, drops it between its legs and runs off. . . . we therefore, wish to remain here, and fight our enemy, if they should make an appearance. If they defeat us, we will then retreat with our father. . . . our lives are in the hands of the Great Spirit. We are determined to defend our lands, and if it be his will we wish to leave our bones upon them.

The speech electrified the Indians, and they were ready to fight. But the British commander believed, probably correctly, that the American fleet could block his supply routes. He felt he had no choice but to pull back inland. Tecumseh's speech had not persuaded the British.

The combined force of British and Indians retreated northward. An American force was now coming after them. The British commander, after wavering, decided to set up his defenses at a place called Moraviantown, on a small river called the Thames (pronounced tems), near the southern end of Lake Huron.

Both the Indians and the British troops were dispirited. The retreat had taken much of the fight out of them. Now Tecumseh's Indians began to abandon him. The confederacy he had so painfully put together was breaking up. At the start of the fighting he had had 1,500 warriors. When he formed them into a defensive line at Moraviantown there were only five hundred left. According to some reports, Tecumseh had a sense that he was going to die in the battle.

His warriors were stationed in a bit of wooded ground between two swamps. It was a good defensive position, because attacking troops struggling through a swamp would make good targets. Then Tecumseh went to where the British troops were waiting. He walked among them, shaking hands with the officers and encouraging the men. When he came to the commander he said, "Father, have a big heart."

The American force in front of them was far larger and included 260 Indians. They had cavalry, too. The battle began with a volley of fire directed at Tecumseh's warriors. Then the American horsemen charged through the woods at the redcoats. The redcoats,

During the Battle of Thames, the disheartened British troops fled, leaving the Indians to battle on alone. The Indians fought bravely but had little hope against the American cavalry.

unable to stand up against mounted soldiers, broke and ran. Some were immediately killed, and the rest quickly surrendered. Shamefully, the British commander, instead of trying to rally his troops, also fled. Tecumseh and his Indians would have to fight on alone.

The American cavalry came at them through the swamp to the Indians' left. As the horses struggled through the deep muck, the Indians shot at them from under cover of the woods. American infantry, too, tramped into the swamp. A group of Indians charged them, screaming their war cries and slashing with their tomahawks. The Americans fell back. But then their reinforcements came up, and drove at the Indians. Back and forth the battle went, the desperate bravery of the Indians alone keeping them in the fight against a much larger enemy. It was hand-to-hand fighting everywhere.

Then, as the battle was raging, an American spotted Tecumseh and fired. The bullet went into the left side of the great Indian's chest, killing him instantly. News spread quickly that Tecumseh was dead. The Indians, deserted by the British, had now lost the man who had brought them together and had inspired them with visions of getting their land back. The heart went out of them. They pulled back. The Battle of Moraviantown was over. Later, many soldiers claimed

Many stories have been told about the death of Tecumseh. In truth, nobody knows who fired the fatal bullet. This is an artist's idea of how the great chief might have died.

to have been the one who killed Tecumseh, but nobody really knows for sure.

The Indians' chances of holding onto their ancient lands in the Northwest Territory were gone. The Prophet tried for awhile to take over Tecumseh's role as leader of the Indians, but everybody knew he was not nearly the great person his brother had been, and they would not follow him. The War of 1812 dragged on with no result until 1814, when both the British and Americans tired of it and worked out a peace treaty.

For a time the Indians went on fighting the Americans. There were some bloody battles. But because the Indians did not fight as one, they almost always lost. Within twenty years most of the tribes of the East were forced across the Mississippi to lands in the West.

There they attempted to make new lives for themselves. Inevitably, the time came when the Americans wanted that land, too. Bit by bit the Indians were driven onto reservations scattered around the West, where they had to learn to live as white people did, farming rather than hunting. In the 1860s and 1870s the Sioux chief Sitting Bull, another great Native American leader, tried, like Tecumseh, to preserve the land for the Indians. Once again the settlers were too strong. Sitting Bull failed as well.

Today Tecumseh remains a great hero, not only to the Shawnees, but to all Native Americans. Canadians remember him as one who helped defend their country when the Americans attacked it during the War of 1812. There is a town named Tecumseh in Canada, and many Canadians have written stories and poems about him. In the United States Tecumseh is remembered as a brilliant leader, and admired as one of the great men of his time who was passionate in the defense of his people.

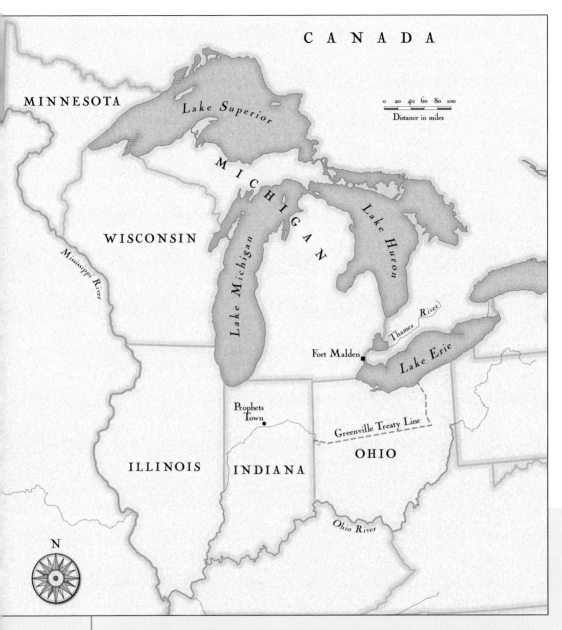

CANADA

MINNESOTA

Lake Superior

MICHIGAN

WISCONSIN

Lake Michigan

Lake Huron

Mississippi River

0 20 40 60 80 100
Distance in miles

Thames River

Fort Malden

Lake Erie

Prophets
Town

Greenville Treaty Line

ILLINOIS

INDIANA

OHIO

Ohio River

N

This map shows the area of the United States that was known as
the Northwest Territory. Tecumseh fought to keep the colonists from
settling the land, but in the end Indian claims would be ignored.

Author's Note on Sources

Because there is so little documented material on Tecumseh's life, there has been surprisingly little written about him from a scholarly viewpoint. Fortunately, there is available one carefully researched biography: *Tecumseh: A Life*, by John Sugden (Henry Holt: New York, 1997).

For students there is *Tecumseh, Shawnee Rebel*, by Robert Cwiklik (Chelsea House: New York 1995) and *Tecumseh and the Dream of an American Indian Nation*, by Russell Shorto (Silver Burdett: Englewood Cliffs, NJ, 1989).

INDEX

ABOUT THE AUTHOR

James Lincoln Collier has written many books, both fiction and nonfiction, for children and adults. His interests span history, biography, and historical fiction. He is an authority on the history of jazz and performs weekly on the trombone in New York City.

My Brother Sam Is Dead was named a Newbery Honor Book and a Jane Addams Honor Book and was a finalist for a National Book Award. *Jump Ship to Freedom* and *War Comes to Willy Freemen* were each named a notable Children's Trade Book in the Field of Social Studies by the National Council for Social Studies and the Children's Book Council. Collier received the Christopher Award for *Decision in Philadelphia: The Constitutional Convention of 1787*. He lives in Pawling, New York.